HAL•LEONARD
INSTRUMENTAL
PLAY-ALONG

AUDIO
ACCESS
INCLUDED

PLAYBACK+
Speed • Pitch • Balance • Loop

TENOR SAX

CHRISTMAS CLASSICS

Audio arrangements by Peter Deneff

To access audio visit:
www.halleonard.com/mylibrary

Enter Code
5053-0456-5533-5357

ISBN 978-1-4950-7057-0

HAL•LEONARD®
CORPORATION
7777 W. BLUEMOUND RD. P.O. BOX 13819 MILWAUKEE, WI 53213

In Australia Contact:
Hal Leonard Australia Pty. Ltd.
4 Lentara Court
Cheltenham, Victoria, 3192 Australia
Email: ausadmin@halleonard.com.au

Visit Hal Leonard Online at
www.halleonard.com

ANGELS WE HAVE HEARD ON HIGH

TENOR SAX

Traditional French Carol

BRING A TORCH, JEANNETTE, ISABELLA

TENOR SAX

17th Century French Provençal Carol

COVENTRY CAROL

TENOR SAX

Traditional English Melody

FUM, FUM, FUM

TENOR SAX

Traditional Catalonian Carol

GO, TELL IT ON THE MOUNTAIN

TENOR SAX

African-American Spiritual

GOD REST YE MERRY, GENTLEMEN

TENOR SAX

Traditional English Carol

HERE WE COME A-CAROLING

TENOR SAX

Traditional

THE HOLLY AND THE IVY

TENOR SAX

18th Century English Carol

I SAW THREE SHIPS

TENOR SAX

Traditional English Carol

JINGLE BELLS

TENOR SAX

Words and Music by
J. PIERPONT

O COME, ALL YE FAITHFUL

TENOR SAX

Music by JOHN FRANCIS WADE

O HOLY NIGHT

TENOR SAX

French Words by PLACIDE CAPPEAU
English Words by JOHN S. DWIGHT
Music by ADOLPHE ADAM

SILENT NIGHT

TENOR SAX

Words by JOSEPH MOHR
Music by FRANZ X. GRUBER

STILL, STILL, STILL

TENOR SAX

Salzburg Melody, c.1819

WHAT CHILD IS THIS?

TENOR SAX

16th Century English Melody